Shall we have Magic?

Alan Baxter

Shall We Have Magic? is a book of beautifully written poems by Alan Baxter. "I usually write about the eternal happenings in nature, but in my poems the Divine turns up in areas not usually expected." This is what Mr. Baxter states in the interview given him in Richard Ramson's documentary *Bohemia: the Life of a New York City Poet.* In Baxter's book you will not only find very interesting poems about nature's grandeur, but you will also find poems about a skewed universe where God's awesome presence can be felt in a college lecture hall gun-downed by an insane young student, in a kinky, raves—after hours NYC party hosted by a suicide-minded doorman, and in the whisperings within "the loneliness of the lover, aching for his passionate partner." Baxter's poetic magic is both shocking as well as exhilarating, yet when the sorcery confronts Ultimate Reality, sparks will certainly fly off into the air.

Contents

The Mystery of Selfhood

Digital Identity

Auden said our identity has become a collection of digits.
But now those digits have taken on an identity of their own.
------And with such power.
They will eventually rule our very world.

In the morning you need a number code to turn on the coffee.
You could not buy your groceries if you forgot your credit card code.
You need those digits to withdraw from the ATM.
Without those numbers, penury you would go.

Those digits allow you to charge up your Holidays
Those digits allow you to buy all your gifts
Yet God forbid if you forgot all these numbers
Only those digits allow you to use the office bathroom.

These numbers allow you to go into your computer.
These numbers allow you to communicate with the rest of the world.
So why are we giving up our rights to these numbers?
Why are we allowing them to direct our very lives?

Here's to you digital identities-----Be gone !!

Am I Alive? Am I Dead?

I put down my iPod
I put my cell phone aside
I unbutton my top shirt
To soak in the morning mist.

I lie in Whitman's scented grass.
I flail my arms in the dewy dust.

I have been in this spot before.
It is a cemetery—pastoral, tranquil
Overlooking righteous, green hills
Grass carpets lit by the rising sun.

I know I was here many years ago
To bury my parents.
Yet I do not know where their gravestone is.

Many monuments scream out
The images of past events.
Buried within these hills are
Revolutionary War Minute Men.
The chapels have seen a parade of bodies
From the canyons of the callous Civil War.

Dead bodies preserved for an After-Life of Splendor?
Rivaled only by the Pharaohs of Egypt?
Lounging undisturbed in these quiet mounds,
Yet hardly ever conscious of the very pristine scenery.

I know that grass and the dust are really
God's Deepest Breath.
And my fondest inner memories
Of my parents' eternal spirits
Are far more precious than their very sculptured mark.

The eerie silence starts to get to me,
As the setting sun against darkened trees
Reminds me of the backlight of a common movie set.

I re-plug my ipod
I pick up my cell phone
I button my shirt

And decide to return to the Land of the Living.
Am I Alive?   Am I Dead?

Cosmos Diner

So why doesn't Joe come home? He's still is at the Diner. Talking about when in high school when he was a big football star in his senior year when he was the most popular student on campus and when they saw him play and they gave him a scholarship to the Big Ten and Joe still talks about him not being able to leave home cause his mother was not well and you know he had some other big deals coming down the line in the next few months so you know he couldn't leave home and that is what he is telling everybody-----the constant revolving doors at the Cosmos Diner. People going in and out--------So Joe is still down there saying how he married me he was going to take me away to the West Coast but yet he wanted to make sure he got the right job offer cause so many important companies were after him and he couldn't decide cause he got so many top job offers and he wanted to make sure he would be able to get that house on the Big Sur and he was so right on when he talked about how he wouldn't be taken advantage of by nobody----------

The constant revolving doors at the diner. Never closing. Open 24 hours a day.-----------

So Joe is still at the diner talking about why he never took the California offer cause something really big was going to happen here in New York and he's not going to waste time with small time stuff and who wouldn't and anyway he's still talkin' about the 100 acres estate upstate someone was going to give him a big deal on and he knew a good real estate agent who was going to give him a good tip and Joe knew the controller up there who was going to bring him in on a great development deal and all Joe needed to do was to put down 100 grand and Joe said that was no problem, but he wouldn't go along with the deal unless he could put a third of it down in cold cash and the rest in bank checks, but he would have to see what bank would give him the right mortgage cause he just wasn't going to deal with any bank------The constant revolving doors of the diner. With people always going in and out. In and out.---------------------but Joe is still talkin' there about that big movie deal and how DreamWorks wanted so much to option that script he owned for the writer knew Joe and only wanted Joe to represent him but Joe decided not to take the deal and you know how Joe's face lights up when he talks about this because the studios didn't know how to produce the high caliber of script he had and Joe only wanted Brad Pitt to play the lead and the studio said Tom Cruise wanted the part so Joe decided to do it himself and he knew about the Wall Street stock deal that some broker gave him a tip-off about and so Joe decided he would wait until the deal came through before he could put the money down and I know Joe is still down there talkin' about some group wanted him in with them to buy Yahoo because they were hurtin' and didn't want to deal with Microsoft------The revolving doors of the Cosmos Diner. Open 24 hours a day. And never, never Closing.

A Day In the Life of Mr. Wright

Everyday Mr. Wright does the "right" things.
He wakes up in the morning, in the right house,
In the right neighborhood,
Having slept on the right mattress, between the right sheets,
Awakening at the right hour, turned on to the right TV show.
And of course, he arises on the right side of the bed.

Mr. Wright takes the right shower,
With the water at the right temperature,
His shower stall built with the right tile,
Bathing with the right soap,
And afterwards putting on the right cologne.

He dresses in the right suit, with the right tie,
Going to work with the right lap-top case
Making sure he has locked his very elegant house,
With the right key.
His wife he divorced many years ago,
Having made the right alimony settlement,
Which gave him complete and sole ownership of the house
Which, of course, was the right thing to do.

Mr. Wright gets into a very good automobile,
Which has the right power steering,
With the right hydraulic power brakes
Allowing him to listen to the right music,
On the right MP3 Player.
And, of course, Mr. Wright always drives
In the right lane.
Allowing all the in-correct drivers
To pass on by.

Mr. Wright had the right job
Working at the right office building,
On the right street.
With the right desk, having a very good view.
He had proper people to work with,
Fellow employees, also dressed in the
Right clothes, who also came from the
Right neighborhoods.
Always saying the right things to him.
Else, he would not tolerate anyone else.
Mr. Wright deposited his money everyday
In the right bank, with the right bank account number,
Doing business with the right investment broker.
Even depositing valuables in the right
Safe-deposit box, with the right safe-deposit number.

He always ate at the right establishments
With the right people, sitting at the right table,
With the right waiter,
In the right part of the restaurant,
Mr. Wright ate the right steak,
Flavored by the right marinade sauce
Finishing dinner at the right time
So he could go home and go right to bed.

Mr. Wright shook hands
With the right politicians,
Voted for all the right laws,
Went to the right church.
In short, he was very right
With the Almighty.

Yet one day---

Mr. Wright made an error
And did a slightly non-right thing.

And THAT has made an eternal,
Fulfilling significance.

Awe --- and then Shock

O Say, can you See
By the Dawn's Early Good Morning America?
The TV so proudly It Shown
All the TV Adds were broadcast full-blown

Mushroom bombs bursting in Air
Till the Dawn's early Light
Yet when we looked at the sky
Through the fog and the smoke
We knew all was right
When we knew McDonalds was there.

O Say, does that Oil Well
STAND---- SO PROUDLY
O The Land of the Free!!
And the Home of the Haliburtons.

New Orleans Will Rise Again

Your cobblestone streets have always cried out with the grief
Of the struggling working man,
Of his families, of his lovers,
And of his buddies.
The pain from poorly paid labor
The pain from the industrial smog
The pain from the creeping crime and poverty
That clogs your hidden alleys
That dampens your frantic festivals and fan-fared funerals
And detours your sexy streetcars.

The pain that echoes in your silky, sad, bluesy sounds
That echoes forth from your bellowing bars
And that screams out within the Creole flavors
Of your unabashed Quarter.

But, you, the Big Easy
Have survived in your glory.

But once again, New Orleans,
Your streets cry out in pain.
Once again you are smitten by nature's taunts
And the whining saxophones and stalwart trumpets
Blare forth lamentations of neglect.

Yet we pray for your recovery
For you,
The proud working class citizenry
Of New Orleans.
Your Great Day of Fame will come about
And you, the Big Easy, will
Continue in your Historic Glory.

Sitting in an Extremely Well-Lit, Comfortable Room

The spurts and crackles of the gas-lit fireplace
Bounce amber beams to the porcelain china.
And the adjoining stucco walls.

While I sit in my cozy, cushioned chair
My taste buds are engulfed by the aroma
Of the gourmet sauce that covers the
Fillet-mignon and the whiff of
The fine vintage wine.

I then stare at the cold darkness outside
Through the ornately draped lattice windows.
The patters of snow on the window sill
Overpowered by the howling of the wind,
Provoking within us those long ago hungers
Of forgotten centuries.

But I am snug in my well-lit room.
Intoxicated. By the delusions of
Warmth that hover so closely all around me,
By the magic of security
I put my whole trust in.

The Siamese cat on the far dresser,
Curled up in its supercilious elegance,
Winks at me.
Only to remind me of what we
Thought was a secret.
But what instead we all know
In the depths of our souls.

Picture-Perfect Day

Green, lush meadows, towering
Sumptuous mountain peaks with
Dotted pines that penetrate
The billowing wombs of clouds.

The dimly heard winds,
The gentle ruffle of maple leaves,
The sweet scents of honeysuckle
 Embrace the aromatic air.
The alluring crown-vetch,
The beaming Black-Eye Susans,
And the lush carpets of daffodils

Custards of brook waters
Glazing over jagged rocks and crystal pebbles

An impeccably designed needlepoint,
Flowering colors stitched into the
Fabrics of grass:
The skirt of any kind goddess
Or anyone's cave wall.

A perfect tapestry that delights us
In the virtual reality of our senses?
Nature's breath
Blowing the world into Technicolor bright?
A vista of a picture perfect day?

Yet such beauty is never without a flaw,
No cloth so taut that it can withstand
The sneers and shreds of devilish demons,
The overlooked shreds that really link us
To our true battered selves.

An inward tapestry is what we really want
That stitches all the parts into a whole.
True Perfection lies
Within the cobwebs of our minds.

Buffy likes to Play

Buffy is born
Buffy is a Sweet-Looking Cocker Spaniel
Buffy's Mother is a Rover
Rover has four other puppies at the same time
Buffy is Happy
Buffy continues to Play with his Four Other Brothers and Sisters.

Buffy is Bought
His brothers and sisters are also bought
Buffy will no longer see his Mother
Yet Buffy has a New Home
Buffy is still quite happy and Buffy continues to Play.

Feeding is at 12 noon.
Walking is at 6 pm----Daylight Savings Time.

The new Owners buy Two other Dogs
One is called Max, the other Charcoal.
Buffy likes to Play with Max.

Whatever the season of the year
Snowy, rainy, cloudy, or blue sky clear
During the different times of the day
Buffy definitely likes to play.

Max likes to Chase cars
One day Max is hit by a Car.
And his leg is Broken
He is taken to the Vet and
Immediately put to sleep

Now Buffy only plays with Charcoal
Yet Buffy is still quite Happy
Buffy and Charcoal grow older

Feeding is still at 12 noon.
Walking is at 6 pm----Pacific Standard Time.

Then one day Charcoal can not rise up to Play.
He is put to Sleep.
But Buffy continues to be Happy.
Now Buffy Plays Alone.
In spring Buffy wants to smell up other Dogs.
In summer, He likes to play in the Water.
In fall, Buffy buries himself in the Crisp, Brown Leaves.
Whatever the season of the year
Snowy, rainy, cloudy, or blue sky clear
During the different times of the day
Buffy definitely likes to play.

Wake-Up Call

The freakish air infused the
Atmosphere of the September morning.
George was sound asleep
In his basement Manhattan apartment in mid-town

Three times the phone rang.
George reluctantly answered it.

"Run-run, George. Get-out. You can come up here."

George was incredulous.

"What are you talking about? You crazy?"

"Haven't you heard? A 747 has just attacked
One of the World Trade Towers."

"That's impossible," George said. "You're playing a joke.
Our defense is the world's best.   After all,
We're God's Chosen Country. The Invincible USA."

George hung up.
He went back to bed.
It was indeed quiet in his place.

30 minutes later.
Three times the phone rang.

"George. This is no joke. Run-run to Grand Central
Before it's too late.
They've attacked both Towers."

George was still incredulous.

"You're still playing a joke.
Why would anyone do this?
We're helping the underdeveloped.
We're saving the world for Democracy."

George hung up.
It was still quiet.
George went back to sleep.

One hour later. Three times the phone rang.

"George, run-run. Get on the train.
We'll meet you in Yonkers.
We'll meet you in Croton.
Just get out of Manhattan.
The Twin Towers have all Fallen.

"But how could this be," George said.
"We're the best loved country.
Look at all we've done.
What other country would airlift candy bars."

"GEORGE, TURN ON THE T.V." screamed the phone.

George reluctantly turned on the T.V.
And what was to be seen.
Carnage galore all over the screen.

He walked outside and saw people running and running.
Swirls of smoke invaded his lungs.

He saw. He gasped. He believed.

Montreal

Enchanted by your naïve nudity,
La ville de plusieur langues
New France dares to bare its small shops and boutique stores
Against the towering monoliths.
Between modest balconies and slender back alleys.

Your honest freedom is intoxicating.

City of the majestic mountain,
Where Jesus looks down from on high
On your everyday happenings.
Where your charming restaurants and museums
Try to hide your naughty night life.

Un ville qui t'envoi au visage ses couleurs.
Vert, bleu, et orange
City of brutal winters
Where mounds of snow can almost touch your high windows.

City of wide boulevards
Where people skate in parks on natural ice.
City of many cultures
As an Hasidic Jew vocalizes Yiddish with a French accent.

The underground cities
A city of politeness which
Heralds forth the roughest of sports.

Immaculate clean summer parks
Giving forth ebullient flavors in spring,
The drumming in the summer
Heard amidst the trees of Mount Royal.

Your glorious summer colors give us strength
To accept your brutal winters.

The charming townhouses
Painted in brash shades on the outside
The circular balconies with wide staircases.

Christmas decorations that never get taken down til Spring.

Neon-Fetish

Racing forwards
Trying to keep pace with the planets
Trying to rewire our deepest insides
Only destroying the mysteries we have neglected
Worshipping instead the wizards we have made.

Grappling with the indifferent ears of computerized faces
Running from doors we're too scared to open
Running through tunnel streaks of colored lights
Dodging the barrages of strangers

Dazzling instead by our flickering animations
Luxuriating mostly in our prefabricated immortality
Letting our techno gizmos turn our solitude into loneliness

Why can't I see the stars?
Why can't I drink of Nature's secretions?
Why can't I touch your warm blooded hands?

Why can't we -----Stop
   And be----Still
    And be ----Aware
     And be----Fearful
  And to feel the inexhaustible Essence of

  NOW

Visage

In every face one sees valleys of concern
Within the cheeks splotches of passion
Within the freckles measures of experience
The upgraded lines, the grooves of human wisdom
The finely curved, yet sensuous lips

In every face there are flashes of anger
Hidden by a civilized veneer.
In every face thwarted ambitions
And bruises of sadness
Buttresses against childhood fancy.
In every face there is a fallen saint.

In every pupil peppered sparks of spirit
In every smile a delectable mystery
In every laughter scary spontaneity
A definite wholeness within all the fragmented lines.

In every face there is a hidden journey,
A closet of infinite thoughts.
Conspicuous blurriness that always confronts us,
In every face the inexhaustible vision of God.

Jonah's Bon Voyage Party

Against the backdrop of a New York City bleeding sky
Stands the Limelight Club
A cathedral of fun and fantasy.

Jonah is the Doorman
Jonah is the Man
You see Jonah if you want to get in
In with the Waves of people,
In to escape into electronic fantasy.

"Tonight—tonight," he shouts to his regular customers
The After-Hours Rave Party is at my apartment.

Like a Chugging Congo train
That whines through the throng, the revelers
All Chant--- "Tonight. Tonight.
Jonah will do it tonight."

"Right on," yells Suzie, the super silicone breasted blond, as she waves her
hands
    Within the frothy hues of the laser lights.

Outside in the streets
The homeless roll their dice
Banking in their slim fate—
One yells to the waiting throng
"Beware of those who work for the Limelight."

Yet the waves of people keep coming on and on.
The whispering in the i-phones gets louder and louder.

"Tonight—tonight, Jonah's Bon Voyage Rave Party is Tonight"
     Cries Hank, the solid steroid stud, as he waxed his way down the floor,
     Weaving through the curving hips.

"Awesome," shouts Butch, the leather dressed sadomasochistic masher,
     Aiming his eyes straight ahead,
     With a look of cool defiance.
But the hours of the club continue.
Animated dancers slither their hips together in
     Sweet sensuous darkness
Like strange passengers waiting for Osiris' call,
Tempered by that cool, cool Techno music.
Dancers move like praying mantises.
As the wandering strobe lights up their festive faces.
While crystal meth, ecstasy, and cocaine
Plot their way through the cavernous rooms.

----"Britney Spears called tonight. Britney Spears called tonight.
She'll make it to the Party tonight."----

The evening pushes on and on, as the spirited revelers
Make their way through the mellifluous moonlight
     Onward to the shadowy sidewalks
     Onward to the ancient streets
     Underneath the bending lamplights.

They move into Jonah's building
Pushing through ancient metal doors
Stepping up the narrow stairways
Onward into Jonah's apartment
With the techno music blaring on
As a ship sailing into the dark seas
Making a path for Jonah.

The hands of the clock moved on restlessly
Towards the time when Jonah would do it.

Will he do it?

"Shit," he said he would do it, mutters Butch, the sadomasochistic masher.

But wouldn't it be right to just continue on?
What about the cocktails, the AZT.
What about the Neverenteens, the Viramunes,
        And the B-6 vitamins?
What about the suffering?
What about the value in life itself?

----"Michael Jackson called. Michael Jackson called.
He wants to know your plans. You better do it when you can.
It definitely can be the Best Show Stopper."
"If you can't do it tonight, then you can do it at Never-neverland."-----

"But where is Jonah? Where is Jonah?
He said he would do it tonight," the crowd voices.

Suddenly Jonah arrives.
Ah—yes—you knew the Man would arrive.
Now Jonah takes charge
Now Jonah wants everyone to see him do it.
Now Jonah turns the light onto himself.
Now the music stops.

True there will be pain.
True, there will be the sour gossips
But get it all now than later

Won't the fact that he now has an audience?
Won't the fact that it will be like a statement?
Won't that be a factor that will definitely make a difference?

Like a sorcerer,
Jonah slowly raises his arms.

Everyone watches in excitement.

Now Jonah swallows the pills
An accidental overdose of aspirin
A mixture of uppers, even a dash of viorex.

But Jonah's pain only gets worse.
Not the physical pain,
But the pain that comes from within.

Jonah screams out in despair.

"He's still alive." Suzy, the silicone breasted blonde, shrieks.
"But he said he was going to do it.
Look, his body's twitching.
You can see his eyes. He's still alive."

"But that's not fair. But that's not fair."
He said he was doing it tonight,"
        shouts Hank, the solid steroid stud.

Run. Run. Everyone runs.
Everybody runs out of the apartment
Like hunted rabbits.

Leaving Jonah to die alone.
But the time had come, or the moment arrived
When you realize that time never flies by,
And even though you think you're at home,
You realize instead that you're always alone.

The words of the homeless trio
Could now be dimly heard.
"Beware of Jonah's party. Beware of Jonah's party
Beware of those who work in the Limelight."

Tigger*

I look up at Tigger's house
On a small hill, overlooking a range of muted mountains
On a day in late summer,
Feeling the impending chill of a not too distant autumn.

I leave my nature hike to visit her
I feel secure entering that hill.

Like Demeter, she guards the farmland grain and peaceful valleys
As she looks with her binoculars at Nature's events.

She gets up to greet me in her usual awkward gait.
Not able to utter the talk that we took so for granted.
But she welcomed me with a big smile
And warmed me with a nice, big hug.
With her sixth sense she peers into my soul.

With faded album photographs, torn coupons, and swamps of old recipes,
She takes me on a virtual tour of her life at Allen road.

I not only marvel at what she remembers.
For her encyclopedic knowledge of every flower in Duchess County
Impresses me as much as her sense of knowing
Exactly when the seasons will change.

Then she sits at the kitchen table, telling me the visit must end
Because of her many back-logged charities that she must answer.
If only I had one ounce of all her compassion and all her love
I would be indeed a richer human being.

I say good-bye to her and look back at her hilltop house.
But the gods of fate never told me
This was the last time I'd ever see her.

She was the Queen of the Salt Point hills
She was my adopted mother.
She is one whose soul rests in God's Eternity.

Barbara "Tigger" Wilde lived in a house overlooking the 120-acre estate hills of Salt Point, New York. After her death, both her daughter and son-in-law, Linda and Michael Kondor, restored her house, making it a private secondary school, called The Ridge School.

Independent Artist

Confrontation was where he stood.
As anger oozed out of him as easily as semen.
Angel was an independent artist
A young man with dreams too elevated to comprehend.

"I'm an independent artist" he would sing with his tangerine smile
At the indifferent passersby.

"I have to sell my songs and my poems myself,
Standing out here on this cold, cold corner.
"So, why don't you buy one of my poems." He yelled out madly.
Why won't people buy my CDs?"
"Just make it all happen. Like magic. Make it all happen."

But that's the hard life of an independent artist.
His unbuckled pants hanging beneath his behind
He ran like a penguin
At whatever pursuits he could find.

Angel was lovable in other interesting ways,
Still a boy in that manly slim body,
Yet carrying that embittered attitude
With his head stuck up his ass.

Staying still in life he could never do
Going 100 miles an hour
In a world too full of Stop Signs.
Still that cocky lovable boy
Underneath his jacket of toughness.

Looking through a window
Of a life that was too short.
But--- what a life.

"I'm an independent artist, so why don't you buy my CDs?"
Just make it magic. Just make it all happen."

But he wouldn't take a nine-to-five job, as people all told him.
Like a knight of honor, he refused to submit to the demands of another.
He was an independent artist who had to sell his CDs.
That was the great dream that he had.

Because Angel could not sell his songs,
Angel took to selling drugs.
He had to survive, to pay for a roof over his head.
So he could pursue his own dreams.

But he sold in the wrong territory.
"No" was a word he could never understand.

One night he was muttering the drugs he was selling,
Next day his body was found dead in the alley.

But a young man having those dreams too elevated to comprehend,
Is what you have to have
When you're an independent artist.

The Mystery of Love

Only a Dollar

"You only have to give a dollar
To feel and touch my sexy body"
The Go-Go Boy mentioned to me in his
Raspy, GI Joe voice
That invaded my eardrums
As he flexed his chiseled muscles
And circled me with his dazzling lap dance.
His tongue licked into my soul
As his peppermint smile
Breathed into my face,
Spiking my sensuality into an
Unbelievable dimension
Too tempting to resist.
Such a delicious, goose-pimpled divine ecstasy.

And all this paradise---
For only a dollar?

I take out my wallet and
Give him some,
As my hands make my way down
His firm, apple-shaped buttocks,
The rippled abdominals in his chest
Championed only by the firmness
Between his legs.
His hard body moved sweetly
Against mine,
Making me realize that I
Really wanted more.
His voice enraptures me again,
"You can feel my body even more
It's only worth a dollar."

Doin' It at Circle Seven

There once was a stand-up named Cecile
Who had all the charm of an eel.
Her jokes not only corny, but also baloney,
But she's doin' it. But where she's doin' it?
She doin' it at the new Circle Seven.

There once was a musician named O'Neal
Whose singing was definitely surreal.
He choked on B-flat, but burped on C-sharp,
But is she doin' it? Yes, she's doin' it.
Where she doin' it? She's doin' it.
At the new Circle Seven.

Now right here, there's a painter named Sybil
Whose paintings are really just dribble.
But she splatters and she spills
But when she does it she's in heaven
Where –of course – where she does it.
At Circle Seven.

Then, God forbid, there's an actor named Wayne
Who certainly was one of no fame.
His body divine, but his acting too sublime.
But he's mouthing it, maybe bluffing it.
But is he doin' it? Yes, he's doin' it.
Where's he doin' it? He's doin' it
At the New Circle Seven.

Are they boozers? Well – no one knows.
Are they losers? Hell No !
So they do it. And why not do it.
It's salubrious. It's groovy.
They're twisting, and they're turning.
Cart-wheeling, spinning,
Reveling, gyrating—
Because it's doin' it, is all that counts.
True, the bread is un-leaven,
But it sure ain't 7-11.
Where they're doin' it.
They're doin' it at the new Circle Seven.

Moon Glow

The glow of the moon sent a telepathy to my soul.
Causing my mind to travel to dimensions beyond.
Yet reveling in Pandora's demons.
Causing me to be frightened.
Sh—sh—said my soul. Listen to the howling dreams.
It can never destroy the bridges you have built.

Now every object that I saw radiated mythic meanings
Causing me to see my relationship with the One.
Such imagination sent a crossword to my mind
Sh-sh—again said my soul. Listen again to the voluptuous murmuring
of the moon.

The moon whispered again into my ear
Murmuring to me more of exotic delights
Sending me into a dimension of delightful lunacy.
Sh—sh—said my soul.
It can never destroy your steel cage of self control.

The glow of the moon sent out bizarre connections
Beguiling tangents, wreaking havoc to secure disciplines,
Radiating mythic meanings to every object,
Evoking voices from the dark, waiting room next door.
Sh-sh—said the soul.
It can only supplement colors to our black and white lives.

Tough Love

Thank God for a thousand and one sensual experiences
A thousand and one biological thrills
Many firm, muscled bodies
All grasped by sensitive hands.

All those perfumed evenings
A thousand and one piercing eyes
Impregnated by bullish cocks
A variety of chiseled faces
Firmly shaped bodies that snuggle up.

Thank God for an array of erotic extravaganzas
Shameless sexuality
Sensual delights that will produce no end.
Each an abrupt meeting you kiss into.

A thousand and one challenges to conquer
A thousand and one challenges that are never vanquished
A thousand and one organic escapades
A thousand and one delectable memories
Always making you come home, begging for more.

Thank God for a thousand and one fluffs of moist hair
A thousand and one lives
Each lived with undaunted passion
Each lived with ruthless defiance.

A thousand and one firm, tough curvatures
A thousand and one taut, sexual instruments to play with.

Boundaries

The shimmering sun skated along the
Silvery surface of the lake,
While phantom trees hovered amidst
Bullets of crystal snow

Cries of joy in the very distant air
Sledding their way down the icy mounds,
With benches buried by turfs of white
Forgotten now by the ploughmen.

All of nature is cold,
As it can be many times.
Everything is settled by this peaceful whiteness
And boundaries certainly exist.

Except for the intrepid forest brook.

Its aggressive waters would not give in
To frozen stillness.
To prove its worth, it
Pushed onward, between the frozen funnels,
As if to remind us it was still alive,
Still gurgling---still warm.

It would not succumb to Nature's settlement
It pushed beyond the white marshes,
It glided down slippery rocks,
Causing ravine icicles to melt.

Yet no one would dare stop it.
Its creative adventurous nature
Was something we could not help but welcome.
A courageous smile that invades our lonely solipsism.

A dangerous example to a very cold world,
But boundaries sometimes are meant to be broken.

Fantasies for Sale

I give you salve for your drowning loneliness.
I am the fingers that titillate your groin.
I resurrect you after the media has buried you.

So why do people call me evil?
Why do people call me Satan?
I am only trying to make you happy
With fantasies for sale.

True, some come to me when they try to forget.
For then, I will completely fry their brain.

I only become dangerous when people deify me,
I only become poisonous when people use me as their couch.

People want me to be the Merlin in their lives.
But they should only swallow me in limited teaspoons.

Warm Hugs

We like to hug our parents.
We like to hug cute bodies.
We all want security.
We all feel loved when we sense the warmth.

We all want a smiling person who will reinforce us.

Yet why do we need those warm hugs?
If God is everywhere,
Then why do we need that touch?

That longing for others causes as to reach out.
That uncertainty in life we can never forget.
That is why we need those warm hugs.
And that is really the mystery of love.

Hubert Higgenbottom's Erotic Afternoon

Coldly shines the afternoon sun on
Hubert Higgenbottom's penthouse balcony,
Overlooking Manhattan.
Hubert stretches out on his
All too comfortable chair
While the wages of life whine serpentine below
Through cacophonous streets and crowded back alleys.
Yet let us not think of that now.
Forget the famines, forget the pestilences,
Forget the contentions of the masses.

Hubert is eating. Eating on his balcony.
Bordeaux and chables line up on his tray
Neatly filled with trios gras and croquet monsieur---
A delicious afternoon snack.
Yet waiting for dessert,
Waiting for cotton candy
Rushing on his way
To be buzzed up soon by the doorman.

Yes, Hubert is waiting
Waiting to fulfill his libidinal longings
Waiting for that exquisite excitement
In daylight's sizzling peak.
Waiting for that liquid ecstasy
That drains through the fingers like
Synthetic waters oozing in a desert oasis.

Yet now Hubert thinks—
Yet in waiting, what about a change
Change the menu.
First the buns, and then the sausage.
Dare to be different, dare to scream,
Dare to dream—Dare to expose those hidden truths.
Do it in the open. Do it on the balcony.
Create a scandal. Put on a show.
Call in the neighbors.

Is it wrong just to change?
Just to get out of the risqué routine.
Wouldn't it be wise to just do it through the cam?
Just to look and not get involved?

Yet is it wrong to embrace sweet emotions?
Is it wrong to kiss the hard, but rain moistened skin?
Is it wrong to lick a tit?
Is it wrong to long for human warmth,
Rather than to long for cyberspace phantoms?
Is it wrong to reveal your naked weakness?

Ah—the doorbell!!
Strike up the band, pull open the curtain
The maker of magic has finally arrived.
What excruciating excitement!
What fabulous fun!
Off with his T shirt. Off with his pants.
Let the naked body glow in its stellar hardness.
Slurping tongues, rippling muscles,
A washboard stomach, bulging biceps,
An erect penis and a tight firm ass.
The onward rush of adrenaline,
Pulsating rhythms, explosive delights,
And then— And then-----
That's It.

He picks up the money.
He goes. He closes the door.
Ever so quietly. Ever so secretly—
Almost as if he never was there.

The show is over. Hubert mopes.

The night starts to creep into the city
As cars stream through the dark streets below
Like furious fireflies.
Hubert's reflection peers
Through the fragmented CNN images
That pixillate across his giant plasma screen.
The waning sun shoots beams
Through the limp early evening clouds,
Reminding us of those threatening words of wisdom,
Reminding us that we are only fleeting glimpses
In a very unreal story.

Hubert falls asleep.

Halloween Love

Amid the roasted autumn branches
In early adolescence
My sexual dreams awakened

Beneath dampened, wooden bleechers
After the football yells and the cheerleading screeches
Gave way to a silent, gothic liquid night.

Your blue eyes and macho redolence
Urged on our lust, unleashing a storm of
Demonic persuasions.

Your finely curved lips,
Matched mostly by your muscular and lean body,
Took control of my heart,
Titillating my reasoning
While the cupid spirits mocked at our taboo love
Through jack-o-lantern images.

Fear of our possible losses
We took shelter in our masks of love.
My feverish restlessness for you
Overpowered the facile facades of
Happy hayrides and fun-filled bobbing for apples.

Yet, we could no longer retreat to those childish games,
To those quick magic moments of innocence.

But now I am free again.
Now in my later years, my addictive
Hunger for you
Has been swept away with the forgotten dead leaves.
Hidden in my brain amidst crevices of delicious memories.

Yet your cool love left me frightened and alone
Only to later open dark dimensions of my soul.
But my waylaid feelings for you
Have since given me now my freedom,
Only to make me realize what
It means to be human.

The Mystery of God

Rainbows in Winter

Colored wheat-chex fields
Layered in rolls of swollen brown valleys
Stripped tree limbs jetting up in the cold misty air.
Then the sky breathes upon the fields
A sudden unseasonable warmth.
And like all the other surprises of life
A sudden storm erupts,
And washes the fields
With sparkles of rain.

But at the storm's end
A ribbon of light
Unravels itself over the red-streaked trees,
And in the moist air
A rainbow appears
As transparent and as frail
As our shimmering visions of love and peace.

And then the rainbow,
Buffeted by the blustery, winter winds,
Vanishes. Before our eyes.

Yet we look to the source of the rain and the rainbow,
Remembering how light came forth
From an almost infinite sky.
We should all be so foolish
As to look for rainbows in winter.

Twinkle, Twinkle, Little Star

Twinkle, twinkle little stars
How I wonder how many you are.
Looking at you in the skies,
Reflects the emptiness in my eyes.

Twinkle, twinkle glorious lights
Bringing our thoughts to greater heights.
When I see your colors so bright
I then will ponder unknown sites.

Twinkle, twinkle gigantic stars
Makes us perceive how tiny we are
Seeming so close, yet being so far
Dwarfs our proud and earthly scars.

Twinkle, twinkle glorious brights
Waiting for eons just to see your lights
Washed over in a brush stroke of all-white sea,
Like looking through a gauze of eternity.

Twinkle, twinkle little stars
You're really not so little, after all.

Whisperings

He is what you can hear, yet not hear
What you can clearly see, yet only in dim reflections
What you can deeply comprehend, yet still
Be puzzled to the utmost.

She is the Whisperings behind the sad thoughts,
The thoughts that lounge around
Like the overdue guest
Resting under the quiet blanket.

He is known in the loneliness of the lover,
Aching for his passionate partner.

She is the Whisperings in the ashy snow
That powders the sleeping fields
The misty whiteness that numbs the
Gaunt, slender, intimidating trees

The swirling silhouettes that
Are the arching, menacing watchdogs
To Infinity's shores.

They are the silence that
Occasionally grasps us, occasionally frightens us,
The Eternal Whisperings,
The quietness, that is louder than
Any of the flashing sounds of today.

Infinite Waves of Being

A friend of mine

                          Told another friend of mine

Of an interesting sight he saw

                          One morning on a forlorn beach

In the more forlorn section of the world.

                   With water laid out against a crest of finitude.

Among the hot white sands

                          Overlooking the abyss of ocean

Lay fragmented fossils,
Torn pages from a very old scriptural text
A rusted, but zero-powered i-phone
An overused latex condom
A Coca-Cola label,
And the battered tip of a misfired missile.

Then in one major

                          Maelstrom Moment

The tumultuous waves splashed upon the shore

               With the water embracing the strangely littered beach,

And redeeming it again into a ubiquitous Whole.

Northern Illinois University, February 2008

Because he was not welcome in our hallow lecture halls,
He quietly instead intruded onto the stage
From behind the screens
Like a phantom spectacle from our dark imaginings.

Thinking that he was a delusion caused by an undercooked
   Piece of beef
We were surprised when he liberated us
From our prison of thoughts,
Thinking that we were content with out test-tube answers.

In a 90 degree angle, he slowly lifted his arm
Like an uplifted steel crane
His Remington 9mm glazing in the shadow light
Mystifying us as to whether it was a toy or a real gun.

Stone faced.
He pulled the trigger.
Aiming in our direction
Snapping us into a jack-hammer reality.
None of our formulas could tell us why he was there,
He was a nuisance we thought we had expunged.

Yet the wailing screams though-out the corridors
And the splattered blood on the cushioned chairs
Will never be forgotten.
His gun shots roared backwards through centuries of
                    Evolved civilizations
The whiff of his ammunition rattled our decorum of reasoning.

Our intellectual journeys will never be the same.

Fiddler's Bridge

Why are we stopping?   Why do you want to get
    Out of the car?"   said   He.

               "I want to hear the Fiddler's Music" said She.

He said, "What fiddler's music?"
               She said, "You know what I mean?   This is
               Fiddler's Bridge."

"Stop your nonsense. Get in the car!"
               "It will only be a matter of minutes.   And
               What's the point of being so prompt if we
               Can not hear those few imaginings."

"But how can you get meaning
From a sound that is nothing?"

               "There is something there. Just quell your
               Thoughts and listen. Listen.   You can hear
               Him play his fiddle. That's why they call it
               Fiddler's Bridge."

You must have had too many martinis
Before we left the house."

"No—No. Don't you understand?"

"Get with it. There's no fiddler there
Playing music."

"But he was killed when he was robbed
Leaving the barn dance on a moon-lit
Night just like now."

"But that was 200 years ago."

"It doesn't make any difference. Even
Though his body was thrown off the bridge,
His music and his spirit still linger because
His killers were never caught."

He said, "That's a fairy tale. A myth, so why
Do you take it so seriously?"

She said, "But fairy tales can become real if
You just let your imagination take over."

"Honey, the motor is running."

"Just a few more minutes----"

"No, I am beginning to get cold, just standing here
Waiting for you."

"But you haven't given it a chance.
"You haven't really tried to listen."

"No." he said.   "And I don't want to be late for
That party."

"Maybe," she said, "I'll stay for a few
More minutes and catch up to you later."

"And walk three miles!!   You'll get killed.
And then they would have to name a bridge
After you."

"But you know why I really want to listen.
The fiddler was just 15 years old. Just like---"

"Stop it. Now you're getting really
Ridiculous."

"But don't you see how those fantasies heal
our realities?"

"Enough. I don't want to be late."

"But just a few more minutes?"

"NO," he shouted. "My motor is running."

She listened.   Then she got into the car.

They both drove off in the automobile.

Leaving behind in the moonlight

Fiddler's Bridge of Clinton Hollow Road.

Give Us More Magic

Please, O God, give us more magic,
But do not give us a miracle.
Walk on water, jump off the Empire State Building,
Transplant in us a new heart, a new kidney
Remove those unsightly wrinkles
And restore in us a smooth, Hollywood skin.
Give us a Tom Cruise model, or Paris Hilton, all neatly wrapped.
But please, O God, please—
Do not allow us to find fulfillment in our worn, exhausted bodies.

Please, please, Oh, God—Give us more magic,
But do not give us a miracle.
Win us the lottery
Feed the Five Thousand
Plus a few A & P Bonus cards
A 401K promotion and a political appointment.
But, please, please—Oh, God
Do not give us the strength
To really look at each other.

Give us that 21 Century Dream House
Plus an all-paid Disney vacation
And a casino bust at Los Vegas
As well as a Wall Street Bonanza.
But, please, please, O God—
Do not give us a miracle.
Do not give us the courage
To become Face to Face with Ultimate Reality.

The End

Author's Biography

Having been a mainstay of the New York City Poetry Circuit for the last ten years, **Alan Baxter** has read as a featured poet in Evie Ivy's Dance of the Word at the Bowery Poetry Club and has also read his material at ABC No Rio, The Green Pavilion, and The Brownstone Poets. He has had his poems published in *Nomad's Choir*, *The Stained Sheets*, and in a new poetry anthology *The Venetian Hour*. Together with its founder Robin Small-McCarthy, he also hosts Kairos Poetry Café, an open arts venue that meets the third Sunday of every month at St. John's Lutheran Church in Greenwich Village, New York.

Mr. Baxter is not only a film-maker who has co-produced many independent films, but he is also the founder of AB Film Productions, which a number of years ago mounted the feature film *Barriers*, which Mr. Baxter personally directed. His play *Juan and Emmett* has been produced in a very small theater here in New York City. He has also taught literature at The College of New Rochelle, Ramapo College, and at Technical Career Institutes.

www.ingramcontent.com/pod-product-compliance
Lightning Source LLC
Chambersburg PA
CBHW032212040426
42449CB00005B/566